What's it like to be a...
NEWSPAPER REPORTER

Written by Janet Craig
Illustrated by Richard Max Kolding

Troll Associates

Special Consultant: Jules Loh, *Special Correspondent, Associated Press.*

Library of Congress Cataloging-in-Publication Data

What's it like to be a newspaper reporter / by Janet Craig;
illustrated by Richard Max Kolding.
    p.   cm.—(Young careers)
    Summary: Follows a newspaper reporter as he covers different
assignments and describes the activities of editors, proofreaders,
and others inside and outside the news room who help publish and
distribute the newspaper.
    ISBN 0-8167-1807-5 (lib. bdg.)   ISBN 0-8167-1808-3 (pbk.)
    1. Journalists—Juvenile literature. 2. Newspapers—Juvenile
literature.   3. Journalism—Vocational guidance—Juvenile
literature.   [1. Reporters and reporting.   2. Newspapers.
3. Journalism.   4. Occupations.]   I. Kolding, Richard Max, ill.
II. Title.   III. Series.
PN4776.P35   1990
070.4'3—dc20   89-34384

Copyright © 1990 by Troll Associates, Mahwah, New Jersey
All rights reserved. No part of this book may be used or
reproduced in any manner whatsoever without written
permission from the publisher.
Printed in the United States of America.
10 9 8 7 6 5 4 3 2 1

What's it like to be a...
NEWSPAPER REPORTER

Hi! My name's Scotty Hansen. I'm a reporter —and it's a job I love!

A reporter just starting out in the newspaper business usually begins as a cub reporter. That's what I am. The stories I write are called general assignments. That means they can be about almost anything! Covering all sorts of stories gives me plenty of good experience.

I like my job a lot. But it's hard work, too. Want to hear about it? This is what my day is like.

Rrringgg!
There's the alarm clock. I'm up early—I don't want to be late. Soon I'm on my way to work.
"Hi, everyone. Scotty's here—never fear!"
"Hi, Scotty."

First, I go to see the city editor. Her name is Willie. It's her job to give the reporters their assignments for the day. She knows where the most interesting and important stories are happening.

For my first story, Willie tells me to find out about a big fire in town. There's no time to lose! "Get all the facts!" calls Willie. "And bring Flash with you."

Freddie "Flash" Johnson is a photographer. He takes the pictures that are often printed along with the stories in the newspaper. He's good at taking all kinds of pictures.

Flash and I hurry to the fire. Flames and smoke are pouring from a big, old building in the middle of town. Police and fire fighters are everywhere.

Right away, Flash gets to work. *Snap, snap, snap.* He's busy taking pictures.

I talk with a few people in the crowd. I try to gather all the information I can. A police officer tells me that the fire started about twenty minutes ago.

Next, I look for the fire chief. He is busily shouting orders to the fire fighters. Before long, the fire is almost out. I ask the fire chief many questions. He tells me the building was empty when the fire started. Luckily, no one was hurt. He thinks an old furnace in the cellar of the building may have caused the fire.

Carefully, I check all my facts. For a story to be complete I always try to find out the answers to these questions: "Who?" "What?" "Where?" "When?" "Why?" and "How?" These are the things people want to know when they read a news story.

I thank the fire chief for his help. Then I'm on my way to the nearest telephone. I must call the news office as soon as possible. When there is time for me to write a story, I always do. But this time the paper needs the information about the fire right away.

I speak to Ned, one of the news writers. I give him all the facts. Then it's his job to quickly write the story, so it can be in today's paper.

Flash hurries off to develop the pictures he's taken of the fire. Then it's time for me to start my next assignment.

This should be interesting. I'm on my way to the city zoo. It seems the zoo keeper has some uninvited guests.

Here they are now—three baby skunks.
What cute babies! They jump and play like kittens. But I'd better keep away from them. This is one time I'd rather not use my "nose for news."

The zoo keeper says the mother skunk made a nest for her babies in an empty trash barrel. No one knew about the nest—until one of the zoo workers tried to clean out the barrel. He got quite a surprise!

The mother skunk ran away and hasn't come back. So the zoo has made a special home for the babies. They will live there until they're ready to be on their own. Then the zoo keeper will take them to a nearby forest to live.

I hurry back to the news office. I'm ready to write all about the skunks and their new home. I think it's a story everyone will enjoy reading.

Look at all the activity here. Everyone is working to meet the deadline. The deadline is the cut-off time for all stories that will go in today's paper. Any news that happens after today's deadline must go in tomorrow's paper.

This editor is hard at work at her computer. On the screen are news stories that are happening all over the world. The stories are gathered and written by companies called news services.

As quickly as a news story happens, it is sent by satellite throughout the world. From the satellite, the story is entered into a computer. When an editor wants to know which world-news stories should go into today's paper, she watches the computer screen to help her decide.

If she finds an important or interesting story, she presses a few keys on the computer, and out comes a typed copy of the whole story.

These busy people are called copy editors. They read each story that will go into today's paper. Their job is to check the spelling, grammar, and content of the story. They also write the headline for each story—that's the big title that catches your eye when you first look at a paper.

After my story about the skunks is read by the copy editors, it'll be automatically set into type. Then it's not long before it will be printed in today's paper.

Come with me. Isn't this an exciting place? It's called the pressroom. And these giant machines are the printing presses. They can print hundreds of newspapers every minute.

Next the papers are loaded onto trucks. Off they go to newsstands and paper carriers all over the city. And soon everyone will be reading today's news.

Well, it's been a busy day. I'd better start for home now.

Wait a minute! Look at that crowd! Maybe I'd better find out what's going on.